The Little Book of

BREXIT
BOLLOCKS

The definitive guide to taking back control
– of your sanity

ALISTAIR BEATON
& TOM MITCHELSON

D1351008

London · New York · Sydney · Toronto · New Delhi

A CBS COMPANY

First published in Great Britain by Simon & Schuster UK Ltd, 2019
A CBS COMPANY

Copyright © Alistair Beaton and Tom Mitchelson, 2019

The right of Alistair Beaton and Tom Mitchelson to be identified as the authors of this work
has been asserted in accordance with the Copyright, Designs and Patents Act, 1988.

1 3 5 7 9 10 8 6 4 2

Simon & Schuster UK Ltd
1st Floor
222 Gray's Inn Road
London WC1X 8HB

www.simonandschuster.co.uk
www.simonandschuster.com.au
www.simonandschuster.co.in

Simon & Schuster Australia, Sydney
Simon & Schuster India, New Delhi

The author and publishers have made all reasonable efforts to contact copyright-
holders for permission, and apologise for any omissions or errors in the
form of credits given. Corrections may be made to future printings.

A CIP catalogue record for this book
is available from the British Library

Paperback ISBN: 978-1-4711-8916-6
eBook ISBN: 978-1-4711-8917-3

Typeset by M Rules
Printed and bound by CPI Group (UK) Ltd, Croydon, CR0 4YY

MIX
Paper from
responsible sources
FSC® C019777

BREXIT MEANS BREXIT

'When I use a word,' Humpty Dumpty said, in rather a scornful tone, 'it means just what I choose it to mean – neither more nor less.'

'The question is,' said Alice, 'whether you can make words mean so many different things.'

– LEWIS CARROLL,
Through the Looking-Glass

LITTLE THINGS TO SORT OUT AFTER BREXIT

Imminent destruction of the
Amazon rainforest.

Melting of the polar ice caps.

Rise of the Far Right.

Global threat from Islamic terrorism.

Possible nuclear war between
India and Pakistan.

Collapse of civilisation as we know it.

Telling your parents you're gay.

STOCKPILING

Jacob Rees-Mogg's Irish bank accounts.

SOVEREIGNTY

The right to eat chlorinated chicken.

EVER CLOSER UNION

A concept originally proposed by
Silvio Berlusconi to a number of partially
dressed nineteen-year-old pole dancers.

ARRON BANKS

A shallow area of the North Sea
where vast amounts of money are
washed up and redirected by the tide
into the pockets of Nigel Farage.

REMOANERS

People who welcome immigration in
towns where they don't have to live.

A SECOND REFERENDUM

God please no.

BREXODUS

Jews fleeing Britain to avoid Jeremy Corbyn.

THE MILKSHAKE DILEMMA

You're standing on a street corner minding your own business and enjoying a Five Guys Banana & Salted Caramel Milkshake when to your surprise along comes Nigel Farage, a man whose politics you detest.

Do you:

a) Shake his hand and wish him a nice day?

b) Politely inform him that he's a despicable human being, but we live in a democracy and it's important to treat one another with respect?

c) Throw your milkshake all over him?

c) is the correct answer.

TO BOJO

To stutter, bumble, bluster, reference Greek
mythology, ruffle your own hair and quote
Latin in order to conceal what an inverted
pyramid of piffle you really are.

ACCESS TO THE SINGLE MARKET

What we already have.

THE POST-BREXIT DIVIDEND

The dividend paid out to shareholders of American companies after they buy large chunks of the NHS.

THINGS THEY WISH
THEY'D NEVER SAID #1

'The free trade agreement that we'll have to come to with the European Union should be one of the easiest in human history.'

– Liam Fox, July 2017

THE SCHENGEN AREA

A ghastly sprawling land mass where people with pastel-coloured jumpers nonchalantly draped over their shoulders and murmuring to each other in many different languages wander across borders into each other's countries, like they're friends or something.

UNITING THE COUNTRY

Agreeing that we hate one another.

IMPACT ASSESSMENT

Peering over a cliff edge and wondering how much of a mess you're going to make when you hit the bottom.

JUNCKER

A term used to describe drinking
heavily in the afternoon till you
can't stand up without being held in
position by two men in grey suits.

Overheard in a bar:

'I've just had my second Juncker of the week.'

'Why don't we take the afternoon
off and go for a Juncker?'

LEAVE

What the UK car industry is going to do.

THE CHEQUERS PLAN

A little-known Agatha Christie novel in which a group of objectionable people wearing what they believe to be relaxed weekend outfits pretend to be fond of the hostess while plotting to murder her.*

* *Spoiler:* In the end, they get her.

THE FULL ENGLISH

Sudden desire by European MEPs to relieve themselves of their breakfasts the minute members of the Brexit Party stand up to make a speech.

FACILITATED CUSTOMS ARRANGEMENT

A hi-tech system whereby guns
can be carried back and forth
across the Irish border.

OVERHEARD ON THE BREXIT BUS

'Shall we stick another zero on that number we just made up?'

THE DONALD TUSK
RESIDENTIAL CARE CENTRE
FOR TRAUMATISED BRITONS

In despair? Waking at 3 a.m. hearing voices saying, 'No deal's better than a bad deal'? Can't stop crying? Inexplicably angry?

If so, you may be suffering from BRTSD (Brexit-Related Traumatic Stress Disorder).

DO NOT PANIC!

Our highly trained team of specialist practitioners are here to help.

Situated in a former Second World War bunker in the east of Poland, our centre offers a wide range of interventionist therapies, including early morning cold plunges, extensive use of emetics and, for the more serious cases, prolonged electroconvulsive therapy.

Remember: we can restore you to your pre-2016 self!

Payment in euros only.

TRANSITION PERIOD

Five hundred years.

THE IRISH BORDER BACKSTOP JIG

A follow-up to the hugely popular *Riverdance*, the Irish Border Backstop Jig (normally performed at night) involves swift movements of the feet while the arms are kept rigidly to the sides due to the weight of the contraband goods being carried.

GONE A BIT
DOMINIC RAAB

Lunatic single-mindedness backed
by unfeasible resilience and
paucity of self-awareness.

FIVE OTHER THINGS AS STUPID AS BREXIT

The Charge of the Light Brigade.

Prohibition.

Subprime mortgages.

Automated checkouts that let you put avocados through as bananas.

Matt Hancock.

FREE TRADE AGREEMENT

A horse painted rainbow colours with an ice cream cone glued to its forehead.

RESPECTING DEMOCRACY

Not having referendums.

A BIT OF A JAPE

Becoming Prime Minister.

NATIONAL HUMILIATION

Nigel Farage.
Jeremy Corbyn.
Boris Johnson.

SMOOTH AND ORDERLY

Hahahahaha
Hahahahahaha
Hahahaha
HAHAHAHAHAHAHAHAHAHAHA

BETRAYAL

Having a different view from someone else.

TREACHERY

Having a different view from someone else
and wearing it on your T-shirt.

ALTERNATIVE ARRANGEMENTS

A phrase used as an imaginary solution to the problem of the Irish border, frequently confused by British politicians with something real.

See also:

'I'm sorry you're dying but don't worry we'll make alternative arrangements.'

THE PEOPLE'S VOTE

Asking the people a second time because
we have a Danish au pair and go to
farmers' markets and we're very
annoyed at the people's failure
to get it right the first time.

ORDERLY DEPARTURE

Bloke at the party who keeps saying,
'Right! Better be off, then,' and is
still there five hours later.

ALASTAIR CAMPBELL

Forget 600,000 dead in Iraq and listen to me tell you what you ought to think about Europe.

REASONS I VOTED REMAIN

My children made me.

My husband and I quite like reading
menus in languages we don't understand.

Massive fan of A. C. Grayling.

Dad lives in Marbella. Want
him to stay there.

Worried we might lose Miłosz because not
only is he a good plumber, he doesn't charge
VAT, works all the hours God sends, and
has become quite a friend of the family.

REASONS I VOTED BREXIT

My wife had sex with a Spanish waiter.

There were only two choices on the ballot.

I don't like Stephen Fry.

I hate Toulouse sausage.

Generally scared.

THE COMMONWEALTH

A bizarre historical anomaly consisting of a largely pointless and nostalgia-driven association of countries that were once part of the British Empire.

Now our future.

HONOURING OUR MANIFESTO PLEDGE

Going down with the ship.

THE WILL OF THE PEOPLE

Hanging.

Flogging.

Waterboarding.

Crumpets.

Leaving the European Union.

THE WILL OF 0.14% OF THE PEOPLE

Boris Johnson.

THINGS THEY WISH
THEY HADN'T SAID #2

'Getting out of the EU can be quick and easy – the UK holds most of the cards.'

– John Redwood, July 2016

THEY NEED US MORE THAN WE NEED THEM

A printer's error for 'we need them more than they need us'.

KEEPING THINGS
ON THE TABLE

In complex negotiations with the
EU, it's important to know what
should be kept *on* the table and what
should be taken *off* the table.

Maybe start by putting your most ridiculous
proposal on the table. When that's rejected, try
putting a slightly less ridiculous proposal on
the table. The other side will demand that you
remove it from the table, so try putting them
at a disadvantage by taking the tablecloth
off the table. If that doesn't work, try taking
the legs off the table. If this still has no effect,
cut the table in two and take your half back
to London. At least you'll have half a table.
And Britain will have kept its national pride.

SMART BORDER

Fictional solution to everyone's
problems. Like Jesus.

TO BE WIDDECOMBED

A form of gay aversion therapy in which homosexuals are transported to Brussels and forced to listen to Ann Widdecombe making a speech in the European Parliament until they renounce their homosexuality.

CHERRY PICKING

Job opportunity for British workers once
we don't have any Europeans willing to
labour in the fields of Lincolnshire for
1p more than the minimum wage.

THOUGHTFUL TWITTER DEBATE

🐦 **Leaver** @Leaver
In my view the EU's Common Agricultural Policy is seriously misguided

🐦 **Remainer**
Replying to @Leaver
Fuck off u stupid cunt

🐦 **Leaver**
Replying to @Remainer
In fact the CAP is just a heap of shit

🐦 **Remainer**
Replying to @Leaver
So are u

🐦 **Leaver**
Replying to @Remainer
Nazi

🐦 **Remainer**
Replying to @Leaver
Gammon

🐦 **Leaver**
Replying to @Remainer
Traitor

🐦 **Remainer**
Replying to @Remainer
Thicko

🐦 **Leaver**
Replying to @Remainer
Go suk on a Belgium cock

🐦 **Remainer**
Replying to @Remainer
Prob taste better than yours

🐦 **Leaver**
Replying to @Remainer
fAGGOT

🐦 **Remainer**
Replying to @Remainer
#homophobia
#youjustdontgetit

🐦 **Remainer**
Replying to @Remainer
U still there?

🐦 **Remainer**
Replying to @Remainer
yOU left?

🐦 **Remainer**
Replying to @Remainer
Hello?

CORBYNISATION

A massive swelling of the ego brought on by hearing repeated choruses of your name being sung by left-wing millennials. The sufferer frequently retreats into a fantasy world of 1970s socialism and takes to hugging members of Hamas in a desperate attempt to avoid answering difficult questions about Brexit.

THE NORWAY MODEL

Being just like the Norwegians.
Only fatter.

OVERHEARD ON
THE BREXIT BUS

'So when we leave, how am I
going to find a cleaner?'

CRASHING OUT

Catatonic state induced by
watching rolling Brexit news.

STRUCTURE OF THE EUROPEAN UNION

The European Union is often accused of being a vast and unwieldy bureaucracy. This is unfair. Just ask anyone who works for the European Council, the European Commission, the European Parliament, the Court of Justice of the European Union, the European Central Bank, the European Court of Auditors, the European External Action Service, the European Economic and Social Committee, the European Committee of the Regions, the European Investment Bank, the European Ombudsman, the European Data Protection Supervisor, the European School of Administration, or the European Personnel Selection Office and they'll tell you it's not true.

JEREMY HUNTISH

When something is so out-of-date and ridiculous it becomes strangely feasible.

For a while.

THE NIGHT OF THE LIVING LIB DEMS

A zombie movie in which a once-dead political party is brought back to life by the horrors of Brexit. In a terrifying scene, the bloodied and rotting Lib Dems, led by an irritatingly pushy Scot in a yellow dress, rise from the earth and lurch down the middle of the road, striking the fear of God into small children, people walking their dogs, and young people in rags begging for help to pay off their tuition fees.

BESPOKE BREXIT

A disaster but a made-to-measure
disaster and therefore better than
an off-the-peg disaster.

THINGS FOUND IN NIGEL FARAGE'S POCKETS

Receipts from a night out in Belgium.

Folded beer mat with Tommy Robinson's phone number.

Vestiges of Donald Trump's DNA.

Handkerchief to wipe away all doubts.

Handy guide to escaping from crashed aeroplanes.

Embers of a burnt cross from Alabama.

Traces of milkshake.

THINGS FOUND IN ARRON BANKS'S POCKETS

Nigel Farage.

HATE ISLAND

Hugely popular reality TV show in
which 67 million people are dumped
on a small island off the coast of France
and invited to love one another.

Leavers and Remainers couple up, put their
differences aside, get into bed together, and
find parts of each other that they like. This
leads to tears, tantrums and a lot of mugging
off, in an increasingly desperate search to
recouple and find someone they can stand.

Who'll get pied? Who'll get to do bits? Does
anyone know where anyone's head is at?

The show rapidly descends into loutish
bantz, bitter recriminations and profound
mutual loathing, and is scheduled to
run for another forty-eight seasons.

A GREEK TRAGEDY

Yanis Varoufakis's leather trousers.

GLOBAL PLAYER

Post-Brexit Britain negotiates
a trade deal with Fiji.

A MANAGED NO DEAL

A no deal departure completely free
of any unpleasant consequences.

See also:

A managed bullet to the brain.

A managed plane crash.

A managed thermonuclear conflagration.

DONALD TRUMP

President who tells twenty-two lies a day, calls Mexicans rapists, locks immigrant children in cages, tells teachers to take guns to school, describes white supremacists as 'very fine people', denies climate change, boasts about the size of his penis, mocks the disabled, sexually assaults women, wants to date his own daughter, believes third-world countries are shitholes, threatens other nations with nuclear Armageddon. And thinks Brexit is a good idea.

THINGS THEY WISH
THEY'D NEVER SAID #3

'Fuck business.'

– Boris Johnson, June 2018

WITHDRAWAL AGREEMENT

What father-of-six Jacob Rees-Mogg
never signed up to.

AIMS OF THE EUROPEAN COMMON RULEBOOK

1. To maintain standards and regulations on all goods and services across Europe.

2. To make sure you can never leave.

CANADA PLUS PLUS PLUS

An unexplained political phenomenon, similar to the Toronto Blessing, in which British politicians are suffused with feelings of euphoria and start believing we can be just like Canada. Eyewitnesses report seeing a blinding light out of which the figure of Guy Verhofstadt descends from the heavens and distributes incredibly generous trade deals to any passing government minister.

THE IRISH

Who cares?

NOTHING IS AGREED UNTIL EVERYTHING IS AGREED

Nothing is agreed.

VOLUNTARY
ALIGNMENT

Choosing to lay down
alongside Boris Johnson.

THE EUROPEAN RESEARCH GROUP (ERG)

A secretive body of extreme right-wing Conservative MPs masked by an innocuous title so as to be thought of as decent, rational, cultured people.

See also:

Adolf Hitler and the 1933 seizure of power by the European Literary Discussion Club.

USING YOUR PHONE
ABROAD AFTER BREXIT

Expensive.

OVERHEARD ON THE BREXIT BUS

'£350 million a week for the NHS?
Christ, that's more than I pay for
my private health cover.'

TONY BLAIR

Love him or hate him, you've gotta hate him.

SIX THINGS LESS EXTREME THAN PRITI PATEL

Chili enema.

Crystal meth.

Amputation without anaesthetic.

Naked bullfighting.

Night out with paratroopers in Aldershot.

Morrissey.

THE BREAK-UP OF THE UNITED KINGDOM

A minor side-effect of leaving the EU.

SHEPHERD'S HUT

Seeking luxurious solitude? A place to relax and unwind in grade-one comfort? An extra space to entertain friends? Or maybe you're a failed prime minister struggling to come to terms with an ill-conceived, ineptly managed decision that is destroying the country you once led?

For just £25,000, a shepherd's hut offers you a place to hide away and bang your head against the walls.

You know you've earned it.

TRANSITIONAL ARRANGEMENTS

Stockpiling Brie and olive oil.

HEALTH AND SAFETY REGULATIONS

A conspiracy by twenty-seven European states to rob the British people of their God-given right to ingest pesticides, have limbs mangled by factory machines, breathe heavily polluted air, and be cared for by junior doctors who haven't slept for three days.

UKIP

Far-Right political
   party that lurched
      so far to the right it

fell

off

the

page.

FREE MOVEMENT
OF PEOPLE

Allowing Philip Green to fly back
and forward from Monaco.

I BELIEVE IN BRITAIN

A fervent incantation chanted by members
of a 21st-century pagan cult who thought
they possessed magical powers.

Cult followers swore fealty to a paunchy,
overweight guru who preached pluck,
optimism and the spirit of do-or-die.
Losing all ability to think rationally, leading
members of the cult would frequently feel
turbo-charged and call for the blood sacrifice
of doomsters, gloomsters and anyone
else still in possession of their senses.

THERESA MAY'S BURNING INJUSTICES

Grenfell.

FRICTIONLESS TRADE

Trade that nobody notices.

See also:

Sex with a tiny penis.

DELIVERING BREXIT

Sixty-seven million people
arguing for twenty years.

THEY DIDN'T UNDERSTAND WHAT THEY WERE VOTING FOR

Remainers' code for 'I don't agree with the result', supposedly brought about by the lamentable ignorance of the electorate, who, on every other occasion they went to the polls, only did so after spending three years taking a degree in philosophy, politics and economics at Oxford.

THINGS THEY WISH
THEY HADN'T SAID #4

'Don't worry, I know what I'm doing.'

– David Cameron, when asked by Michael
Gove whether a referendum was a good idea

THE METROPOLITAN LIBERAL ELITE

Smug, patronising, know-it-all city-dwellers, poncing around with their university educations, exchanging ideas, reading books, learning from history, trying out foods that normal people wouldn't touch, standing around at cocktail parties thinking they're special just because they know which way to hold their vol-au-vents, experimenting with drugs, changing from men into women and back again, going to the theatre when it's not even a musical, talking to foreigners like they're the same as us, using filament bulbs to light their kitchens, laying wooden floors instead of carpets, going to psychotherapists, looking healthy well into their fifties, doing

Pilates all over the place, recycling their jumpers, wearing trainers with their suits, using Apple watches to count how many steps they've taken, eating vegetables day and night, knowing someone who knows Jeremy Corbyn, changing their minds just because the facts have changed, looking down on people who're stupid, being sniffy about plastic straws, composting their avocado skins, cycling everywhere, being emotionally sensitive, taking the fucking train to Spain when they could fly Ryanair, driving around in some stupid electric car, and taking their babies along on protests against Brexit.

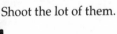 Shoot the lot of them.

OVERHEARD ON
THE BREXIT BUS

'Gosh, I can't remember when I
was last on a bus, can you?'

MOGGSTERS

Similar to fans of the 1980s pop group
Bros, but without the intellectual clarity.

BRITISH RULES FOR NEGOTIATING WITH THE EUROPEAN UNION

- Don't send anyone who knows how the EU works.

- Don't take notes; it only makes the other side think you care.

- Break your promises; just because you've agreed to something, doesn't mean you have to do it.

- Every half hour, threaten to leave without a deal (try not to look scared as you do this).

- If it gets difficult, hold your hands over your ears and shout 'la la la'.

- If they start speaking French, walk out.

GOVING

The practice of snorting a drug that makes the user even more relentlessly loquacious, enthusiastic and unbearable than he was before.

For further reading, see Lord Byron's 'So We'll Go No More a Goving'.

QUESTIONS VOTERS ASKED THE DAY AFTER THE REFERENDUM

What happens now?

Are we still allowed to go on holiday?

Why was I born British?

Can I get an Irish passport?

Where's David Cameron?

THE IRISH BORDER

Shit, we forgot about that.

STREAMLINED CUSTOMS ARRANGEMENT

Funnelling the massive queues.

DEUTSCHLAND DISORDER

A deep fear among Britons that the European Union is run from Berlin and that leaving it is a re-run of the Second World War. Extreme manifestations of this include massive deployment of hissy fits against EU bureaucrats as a substitute for bombing the shit out of Berlin.

THE EUROPEAN UNION'S FOUR FREEDOMS

Freedom to erect hugely expensive and ugly buildings in the middle of Belgium.

Freedom to use impenetrable bureaucratic jargon.

Freedom for MEPs to travel everywhere First Class.

Freedom to fuck Greece.

THE DUP

EU-hating, gay-hating, God-loving, climate-change-denying Northern Irish political party happy to prop up the British government via the arrangement known as 'confidence and supply'.

(The confidence of having Jesus as one of your closest advisers and the ability to supply large amounts of rank prejudice.)

GRAYLING'S DISEASE

Giving large sums of money to
ferry companies without first
checking that they have a ferry.

NO DEAL IS BETTER
THAN A BAD DEAL

A fib.

TAKING BACK CONTROL

... and handing it to Dominic Cummings.

PROJECT FEAR

Making a ridiculous fuss about something
that carries no risk whatsoever.

Of course the British car industry
will survive Brexit.

Of course the banks won't
move to Frankfurt.

Of course we won't have a
fall in living standards.

Of course little Timmy can put
his hand in that blender.

QUESTIONS THAT VOTERS NEVER ASKED

How's this going to work, then?

QUESTIONS THAT POLITICIANS NEVER ASKED

How's this going to work, then?

EXPERTS

'People in this country have had
enough of experts.'

– Michael Gove, June 2016

Scientists, engineers, doctors, lawyers,
plumbers, electricians, economists,
professors, farmers, geologists, accountants,
fishermen, dentists, pharmacists, midwives,
surgeons, sociologists, journalists, teachers,
judges, biologists, musicians, psychologists,
translators, botanists, meteorologists,
physicists, and pretty much anyone else
who knows a lot about something. Who
the fuck do these people think they are?

THE EUROPEAN COURT OF HUMAN RIGHTS

Nothing at all to do with the European Union but has the word European in it and is therefore a threat to everything we hold dear.

REMAINING IN THE EU

Better to be inside the tent pissing over everyone than outside shitting ourselves.

JOBS-FIRST BREXIT

A Brexit where the only thing on the minds of politicians is what position to adopt on Brexit that will guarantee them jobs in the next Cabinet.

MAX FAC

Short for Maximum Facilitation, Max Fac
is a new form of mindfulness in which
technology not yet invented becomes
so powerful an idea in the mind of
the negotiator that all thought ceases
and there is no longer any boundary
between imagination and reality.

TIM MARTIN, CHAIRMAN OF WETHERSPOONS

Ardent Brexiteer who's no longer
allowed near the kitchens in his
pubs in case he gets fried and served
with a pineapple ring on top.

THE BREXIT PARTY

First political party with a manifesto
shorter than its name.

GREAT POWER

Following Brexit, Britain will once again be a great power, as we were in the glory days of empire.

In order to achieve this, we will need to remove ourselves from the world's largest trading bloc, negotiate 179 new treaties with 140 countries, pay the EU £39 billion, conquer Africa, re-establish the Raj, invade Hong Kong, control the world's ivory trade, and dig up Sir Francis Drake.

HAVING YOUR CAKE
AND EATING IT

Boris Johnson's approach to the
European Union. And marriage.

WTO

Like WTF but worse.

USEFUL WORDS AND PHRASES FOR TRAVEL IN THE EU AFTER BREXIT

In the nine-hour queue at immigration: 'Let me through please, I've taken back control.'

At the bureau de change:
'What? Ten pounds for one euro?'

Arriving at your hotel: 'We have a reservation in the name of Smith for the tent in the garden.'

At the tourist information office:
'Is there someone here who speaks English and can explain the backstop?'

At the pharmacy: 'Do you have something to stop this awful feeling of regret?'

POLITICAL DECLARATION ON FUTURE RELATIONSHIP

I won't come in your mouth.

BREXINO

Tiny, tiny, tiny, tiny, tiny Brexit.
Like a pledge not to visit Bruges.

VASSALAGE

What Boris Johnson did to his fag.

USEFUL WORDS AND PHRASES FOR TRAVEL IN THE EU

French verb: *farager* – to soil the public discourse.

Overheard in Paris:

'Ah, mon Dieu! J'ai faragé dans mon pantalon.'

BREXOTICISM

A form of sexual fetish in which gratification is
linked to symbols of Britain's glorious imperial
past, such as Nelson's eye patch, portraits
of Sir Walter Raleigh, and any collection
of poems by Rudyard Kipling. In extreme
cases, the fetishist will experience priapism
in the presence of the Prince of Wales.

Fetishists may also on occasion orgasm
to the sound of Elgar, and are best
avoided at Last Night of the Proms.

THE BREXIT BUS

Thank God two of them don't
come along at the same time.

QUESTIONS ASKED BY EU CITIZENS LIVING IN THE UK

What did I do wrong?

THINGS THEY WISH
THEY'D NEVER SAID #5

'The day after we vote to leave,
we hold all the cards and we can
choose the path we want.'

– Michael Gove, April 2016

ESTHER McVEYISM

A form of amnesia that prevents the sufferer
from realising she's in the wrong profession.

REESMOGRIFICATION

A form of post-Brexit gentrification that produces entire neighbourhoods in which children wear top hats, horse-drawn Ubers trot up and down the retro-cobbled streets, teenagers wobble along on penny-farthings, pop-up emporia on every corner sell only monocles, and excessively courteous young men in double-breasted suits cajole pretty young women into unwanted pregnancies.

ENEMIES OF THE PEOPLE

The people.

BLIND BREXIT

Running your hands at random
over Nigel Farage's face.